Gifts from the Kitchen
CANDY COOKBOOK

by Mildred Brand

A little something,
        Smooth and sweet
For happy times.
        A dreamy treat.

Bits of love for
        Special days.
Touched with mint
        And filled with praise.

Clustered, sparkling
        Gems to cook
Wait within this
        CANDY book.

                    Alice Leedy Mason

ISBN 0-89542-881-4 100

CENTERS

DIPPING IN CHOCOLATE-FLAVORED COATINGS

The recipes in this cookbook, which call for dipping chocolate, utilize chocolate-flavored coatings. If you use real chocolate, it must first be tempered.

To prepare the chocolate-flavored coatings for dipping candy centers, follow these steps:

1. Heat water to boiling in bottom of double boiler (without chocolate near stove).

2. Remove water from heat; place top of double boiler with chopped block chocolate or wafers in it above hot water.

3. Stir occasionally, until chocolate is melted (about 3 to 5 minutes).

4. Remove chocolate from hot water and allow coating to cool for 10 to 20 minutes; or put chocolate over cold water and stir until it thickens slightly.

5. Replace hot water with warm water in bottom of double boiler.

6. When chocolate has thickened slightly, place it over warm water and it will be ready to dip. If chocolate is too thick to dip centers, warm water a little. If chocolate is too thin, replace water with cooler water. Lukewarm water should keep chocolate the right temperature (98°) for dipping.

7. Keep chocolate stirred while dipping.

MAPLE CREAMS

1 c. coffee cream
2 c. maple syrup
Sweet milk chocolate, melted

Cook cream and syrup to 238°. Pour on a cold slab; cool to lukewarm. Work with spatula or paddle until mass holds its shape. Form into ¾-inch balls and dip in melted chocolate. Makes about 25 centers.

PEPPERMINT PATTIES

2 c. Basic Fondant (p. 4)
¼ t. oil of peppermint
Few drops green food coloring
Melted semisweet chocolate

Work Basic Fondant until softened. Add oil of peppermint and food coloring. Form into 1-inch balls and flatten each into patties. Dip in melted semisweet chocolate.

Pictured opposite:
Peppermint Patties, Maple Creams
Orange Pecan Creams, p. 4

BASIC FONDANT

An excellent all-purpose cream center, creamy off-white in color. Rich and smooth.

- 5 c. sugar
- 1 c. whole milk
- 1 c. heavy cream
- 4 T. butter or margarine
- ½ t. cream of tartar
- 1 t. orange, vanilla, or almond flavoring (optional)
- 1 c. chopped nuts (optional) Dipping chocolate

Combine all ingredients in a large saucepan. Stir until sugar is moistened. Place over high heat. It is not necessary to use a lid. Bring to a boil, then gradually lower candy thermometer into boiling syrup. Cook without stirring, lowering the heat slightly as mixture thickens. Cook to 236°. Pour out on a slab and cool to lukewarm. Work with spatula until fondant creams, then knead with hands until it is very smooth, adding a flavoring or chopped nuts, if desired. Form into a ball and let rest on the slab until it is completely cool. Form into ¾-inch balls and dip in chocolate. It is better to let fondant ripen a few days, then form and dip the centers. To store, wrap tightly in waxed paper or plastic wrap, place in a bowl and cover with a damp cloth. Makes about 125 centers.

ORANGE PECAN CREAMS

- 2 c. Basic Fondant
- ¾ t. oil of orange
  Few drops orange food coloring
- ½ c. finely chopped nuts Dipping chocolate

Work Basic Fondant until softened. Add oil of orange, food coloring and chopped nuts. Blend all together. Form into ¾-inch balls and dip in chocolate.

COCONUT CENTERS FOR BONBONS

- ¼ c. corn syrup
- 6 large marshmallows, quartered
- 1 c. desiccated or macaroon coconut
- ½ t. vanilla

Melt syrup and marshmallows over medium heat. Remove from heat; add coconut and vanilla. Let set until cool enough to handle, then shape into ¾-inch balls. Makes about 20 centers.

DIPPING BONBONS

Heat coating slowly in upper part of double boiler until it melts to the consistency of heavy cream. Do not stir more than necessary. Keep fondant over hot water or work at the stove. With fork, coat bonbon centers. Drop on waxed paper. These do not keep long.

VANILLA BUTTERCREAMS

Special center with a fresh butter flavor. Good, good!!

- 3 c. sugar
- 1 c. water
- ¼ t. cream of tartar
- ½ c. butter, broken into little pieces
- ¼ t. salt
- 1 t. vanilla
  Dipping chocolate

Combine sugar, water, and cream of tartar in a saucepan; cover with a tight lid and cook. When steam runs down sides of pan, remove lid and cook to 238°. Pour out on cold slab and let stand until lukewarm. Place butter pieces, salt, and vanilla over the syrup and work with spatula or paddle until fondant is cool and thick. Move to a cooler part of the marble slab or other cold surface and let stand until candy is firm, holds its shape and is not sticky. Knead for a moment or two until creamy. Wrap in waxed paper and store in refrigerator until very firm, then shape into ¾-inch balls. Let stand about 30 minutes before dipping; for best results, dip within 2 hours. If kept longer than a week, wrap well and freeze. Makes about 60 centers.

CHOCOLATE FONDANT

A deliciously chocolate-flavored center, quite firm.

- ¾ c. water
- 3 1-oz. squares baking chocolate
- 2 c. sugar
  Dash of salt
- 2 T. corn syrup
- ½ t. vanilla

Combine water and chocolate in a deep 2-quart saucepan. Place over low heat and cook until blended, stirring constantly. Add sugar, salt, and syrup. Stir to mix ingredients thoroughly. Place a tight lid on pan and cook until steam comes from under the lid. Remove lid and cook without stirring to 236°. Pour on cold slab and cool to lukewarm. Work with spatula until creamy, then knead with hands, until smooth. Add vanilla, working it in with spatula. Let stand, uncovered, until cold. Wrap in waxed paper and use as chocolate centers. Makes about 50 centers.

MINTS

MINT SANDWICH

Chocolate-green-chocolate layered mints. Very pretty and good, too.

3½ c. semisweet chocolate coating, finely chopped or wafers
2 c. green chocolate coating, finely chopped or wafers
2 T. coconut oil or vegetable shortening, divided
Few drops of peppermint oil

Melt chocolates in separate double boilers over hot, not boiling water. Add 1 tablespoon coconut oil to each pot of chocolate. Flavor green chocolate with peppermint oil. Cool both coatings down to between 85° to 90°; keep warm water in the bottom of the double boilers. Thinly spread one-half of the dark chocolate over waxed paper. Wait until layer is just about firm, then spread the entire pot of green chocolate thinly over all of the chocolate layer. Again, wait until green layer is almost firm, then spread remaining semisweet chocolate over the top. Let the candy harden, then cut with a sharp knife dipped in hot water and dried. Can build up several layers if desired, and different colors can be used. Makes about 60 squares.

MINTS MADE FROM ICECAP COLORED COATINGS

Mints made in this way are simple to make and very delicious.

Melt 1 lb. colored chopped coating over hot (not boiling) water in a double boiler. When melted and smooth, add 2 or 3 drops of peppermint oil to the chocolate (vary the amount according to taste.) By using a spoon or a candy funnel fill the cavities of a mold (using soft rubber and clear plastic molds). Be careful not to overfill and tap mold to release air bubbles. Place mold in freezer for a few minutes, then remove candy. It is not necessary to grease or prepare the molds in any way. Any flavoring oil can be added to the chocolate to make good candies other than peppermints. Makes 50 roses and 75 to 80 leaves.

*Pictured opposite:
Mint Sandwiches, Mints made from
Icecap Colored Coatings*

MELTAWAY MINTS

Peppermint-flavored square chocolate mints to be dipped.

- **1½ lbs. dipping chocolate, finely chopped (milk, semisweet, or mixture)**
- **⅔ c. melted vegetable shortening**
- **3 or 4 drops oil of peppermint (or to taste)**
- **Dipping chocolate**

Melt 1½ lbs. of dipping chocolate over hot water in a double boiler. Beat until smooth. Add shortening, beating until just blended. Pour into a small bowl and chill in refrigerator until the consistency of soft custard. Occasionally scrape from the sides and bottom of the bowl. Beat with an electric mixer about 30 seconds. Do not overbeat. It will appear lighter in color and texture. Mix in peppermint and pour out on a waxed paper-lined 10 x 13-inch pan. Place a piece of waxed paper on top of batch and level off. Let stand in a cool place until firm but not hard. Cut into squares; leave in the pan until ready to dip. Makes about 80 pieces.

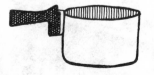

BAVARIAN MINTS

Light flavored and light textured, melt-in-your-mouth chocolate mints.

- **1¼ lbs. chocolate coating (sweet, semisweet, or a combination)**
- **4½ c. dry fondant (p. 20)***
- **2½ T. light corn syrup**
- **1 c. evaporated milk**
- **½ t. invertase**
- **⅛ t. peppermint oil**

Melt chocolate in a double boiler. Combine dry fondant, corn syrup, evaporated milk, invertase, and peppermint oil, and beat on high speed of electric mixer 12 to 15 minutes. Gradually add the melted coating, beating at medium speed. When all is added, whip at high speed for 30 seconds, then spread out in a 10 x 15-inch buttered pan to set. Cut into squares. Makes about 90 pieces.

CARAMELS

CREAM NUT CARAMELS

Nut-filled and chewy.

- 1 c. heavy cream
- 1 c. coffee cream
- 2 c. sugar
- 1 c. light corn syrup
- ¼ c. butter
- ½ t. salt
- 1 t. vanilla
- ½ c. chopped pecans

In a small saucepan, combine heavy cream and coffee cream; and warm. Place one cup of the cream mixture into a 4-quart saucepan, add sugar and syrup. Cook for about 5 minutes. Very slowly add the remaining cream mixture so that boiling does not stop. Cook about 5 more minutes. Add butter, small amounts at a time; and cook slowly to 244° to 246°. Watch thermometer during cooking; when it reaches 230°, lower heat to prevent scorching. If a heavy saucepan is used, no stirring should be necessary. When thermometer reaches 244° to 246°, remove candy from heat and let stand 10 minutes. Carefully stir in salt, vanilla and pecans. Pour into a well greased 8-inch square pan. Let stand until firm, then cut into squares and wrap. Makes about 49 pieces.

CARAMELS

Just two main ingredients. Stir well a few minutes as they cook and you have another very good caramel.

- 1 15-oz. can sweetened condensed milk
- 1 c. light corn syrup
- ¼ t. salt
- 1 t. vanilla
- 1 T. butter

Combine milk, corn syrup, and salt in a heavy pan; bring to a boil over medium heat, stirring constantly. Cook, stirring constantly, to 240° to 245°, depending on the firmness of the caramel desired. Remove from heat, add vanilla and butter. Blend well and pour into a buttered 8-inch square pan. Cool, cut, and wrap. Makes about 36 pieces.

Note: This candy scorches easily. If small brown spots appear, continue to stir rapidly. This will dissolve spots into the candy as it continues to cook.

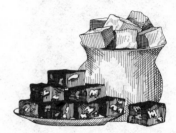

BLACK WALNUT CARAMELS

3 c. brown sugar, packed
2 c. light corn syrup
1 c. butter
¾ c. sweetened condensed milk
½ t. vanilla
1⅓ c. black walnuts

Combine sugar, corn syrup, butter, and condensed milk in a heavy pan. Cook over medium heat, stirring constantly, until sugar is dissolved and mixture boils. Continue cooking to 248°, stirring now and then to prevent scorching. Remove from heat and stir in vanilla and walnuts. Pour into two buttered 8-inch square pans. When firm, cut and wrap in waxed paper squares. Best stored in refrigerator. Makes about 98 pieces.

HONEY CARAMELS

1¼ c. sugar
1½ c. heavy cream
½ c. honey
6 T. flour
6 T. butter
1 t. vanilla
1 c. chopped nuts

In a large saucepan, combine sugar, heavy cream, honey, flour and butter. Cook stirring constantly, to 245°. Remove from heat; stir in vanilla and nuts. Pour out into a buttered 8-inch square pan. Cut into squares when cool. Makes about 30 pieces.

CARAMEL-COCONUT ROLL-UPS

⅓ c. invert sugar
1 c. light corn syrup
2½ c. liquid non-dairy coffee cream, divided
1¼ c. heavy cream
2¼ c. sugar
5 T. butter
½ t. salt
1 t. vanilla
Coconut Bonbon recipe (p. 4), tripled

Combine invert sugar, syrup, ¼ cup coffee cream, heavy cream, sugar, and butter in a saucepan. Bring to a rolling boil. Add remaining coffee cream slowly so boiling does not stop. Cook without stirring to 245°. Turn heat down a little as mixture thickens. Remove from heat and stir in salt and vanilla. Pour into a 9 x 13-inch pan. When cool and firm, turn out on a greased marble slab. Distribute prepared Coconut Bonbon evenly over the top of the caramel. Roll tightly together. Stretch the roll to the desired diameter. Slice and wrap the pieces. Makes about 70 pieces.

Pictured opposite:
Black Walnut Caramels, Honey Caramels, Caramel-Coconut Roll-Ups

FUDGE

THREE LAYER FUDGE

An easy, attractive candy with a white center layer.

- ¾ c. butter, divided
- 1 1-oz. square baking chocolate
- 1¼ c. sugar
- 2 t. vanilla, divided
- 1 egg
- 2 c. crushed graham crackers
- 1 c. flaked coconut
- ½ c. nuts
- 2 T. light cream
- 2 c. confectioners' sugar
- 6 oz. (1 generous cup, un-melted) semisweet chocolate
- 3 T. paramount crystals (optional)

Melt ½ cup butter and baking chocolate. Blend in sugar, 1 teaspoon vanilla, egg, graham crackers, coconut, and nuts. Mix well with a spoon, then with hands. Press mixture in an ungreased 11½ x 7½ x 1½-inch pan; refrigerate. Mix together ¼ cup butter, light cream, confectioners' sugar, and 1 teaspoon vanilla; beat well. Spread over chocolate mixture in pan; chill. Melt semisweet chocolate and paramount crystals over hot, not boiling, water. Spread melted chocolate over white filling; chill. Cut into 1-inch squares. Store in refrigerator. Makes about 56 pieces.

COFFEE FUDGE

A mildly flavored fudge for coffee lovers, topped with chocolate and nuts.

- 3 c. sugar
- ¾ c. milk
- 2 T. instant coffee powder
- ½ c. non-dairy liquid coffee cream
- 1 T. light corn syrup
- 2 T. butter
- 1 t. vanilla
- 1½ c. (6 oz.) chopped chocolate coating or wafers
- ¼ c. finely chopped nuts

Combine sugar, milk, instant coffee, coffee cream and syrup in a 3-quart saucepan. Cover and bring to a boil. Uncover and place thermometer in pan; and cook without stirring to 236°. Remove from heat; add butter and vanilla without stirring. Cool to lukewarm. Beat until candy begins to thicken; pour into a buttered 8-inch square pan. Melt the chocolate coating over hot, not boiling, water in a double boiler. Spread evenly over fudge, sprinkle nuts over chocolate. Cut into squares before candy becomes firm. Makes about 49 pieces.

WHITE FUDGE

1⅓ c. sugar
½ c. butter or margarine
⅔ c. non-dairy liquid coffee
  cream
⅛ t. salt
½ lb. white chocolate coating
  (wafers or block chocolate,
  finely chopped)
2 c. miniature marshmallows
½ t. vanilla
  Dipping chocolate (optional)

Cook first 4 ingredients without stirring to 238°. Remove from heat and add the next 3 ingredients. Blend well. Pack into a 9-inch square pan. When partially cool, cut into squares. Other colors of chocolate (pink, green, yellow, butterscotch) can be added instead of white, adding appropriate flavoring, fruits or nuts. The fudge can be packed in pans and cut in squares or bars, or rolled in a log and sliced, then dipped in chocolate. Makes about 64 pieces.

FRENCH CREAM
ALMONDINE

5 c. chopped milk chocolate
½ c. milk
¾ c. marshmallow creme
2½ c. chopped toasted almonds,
  divided

Melt milk chocolate to 110°. Scald milk. Add hot milk and marshmallow to melted chocolate, beating until smooth. Stir in 1½ cups almonds. Spread in a buttered 8-inch square pan. Sprinkle remaining almonds over top and press in. When set, cut into squares. Makes about 49 pieces.

COCOA FUDGE

A good basic chocolate fudge. The use of whipping cream or non-dairy cream substitute makes stirring unnecessary. This makes a very creamy fudge.

⅔ c. cocoa
3 c. sugar
⅛ t. salt
1½ c. heavy cream or non-dairy
  liquid cream substitute
¼ c. butter
1 t. vanilla

This fudge Stay's gooey doesn't set up

Combine cocoa, sugar, salt, and heavy cream in a large saucepan. Bring to a rolling boil; then reduce heat to medium and cook to 234° without stirring. Remove from heat and add butter and vanilla. Do not stir. Cool to lukewarm (about 110°). Beat by hand or with mixer until fudge thickens and loses some of its gloss. Quickly spread fudge in lightly buttered 8-inch square pan. When cool, cut into squares. Makes about 49 pieces.

CRUNCHY CANDY

ROCK CANDY

Flavorful, colorful, hard candy. Use for suckers or cut into small pieces.

1¾ c. sugar
½ c. water
½ c. light corn syrup
Dash of salt
Food coloring as desired
¼ t. flavoring oil
Confectioners' sugar

In a small saucepan, combine sugar, water, corn syrup, and salt and stir until sugar dissolves. Cover and bring to a rolling boil. Remove lid, place thermometer in pan and cook to 250°. Add food coloring and continue cooking to 300°. (Remove from heat at 285° to 290° as temperature will continue rising to 300°.) Let cool a few minutes. Add flavoring oil and cover 5 more minutes. Pour into a butterd 7 x 10-inch pan. Cut with shears into strips as soon as cool enough to handle. Then cut into squares or diamond shapes. When cold, dust with confectioners' sugar to keep from sticking. Makes about 50 small pieces.

Note: To form suckers, spray rubber molds with vegetable coating and pour hot syrup in. Unmold when cool.

BUTTER-NUT CRUNCH

An excellent toffee, crunchy sweet. Try it with pecans or pecan substitutes.

1 c. sugar
½ t. salt
¼ c. water
½ c. butter
½ t. lecithin
½ c. nuts
3 c. sweet chocolate, melted

Combine sugar, salt, water, butter and lecithin in a heavy skillet or saucepan. Cook to 285°. Add nuts. Pour onto well greased cookie sheet; cool. Spread half of sweet chocolate on the cooled candy. Sprinkle with nuts. When the chocolate is firm, turn the candy over on waxed paper and spread with remaining melted chocolate. Sprinkle with remaining nuts. Break into pieces when firm. Makes about 20 pieces.

Pictured opposite:
Butternut Crunch; Almond Nougat, p. 17
No-Cook Marshmallows, p. 19

SISTER MABEL'S SUPER CARAMEL CORN

2 c. light brown sugar
½ c. light corn syrup
1 c. butter or margarine
¼ t. cream of tartar
1 t. salt
1 t. baking soda
6 qts. popped corn

In a saucepan, combine sugar, corn syrup, butter, cream of tartar, and salt. Boil rapidly on medium high heat, stirring constantly, until mixture reaches 260°. Remove from heat. Stir in soda, stirring to mix thoroughly. Immediately pour over popped corn in a large bowl, stirring until well coated. Place coated corn in a large buttered roasting pan or sheet cake pan. Bake caramel corn for 1 hour in a preheated 200° oven, stirring 3 or 4 times. Keep in a tightly covered container. If it becomes sticky, place in oven again for a little while. Makes about 6 quarts.

PEANUT BRITTLE

3 c. sugar
1¾ c. light corn syrup
1 c. water
5 c. (1½ lbs.) raw peanuts
2 T. butter
¾ T. baking soda
1 t. salt

Cook sugar, corn syrup, and water to 240° and add peanuts. Cook to 295° stirring constantly. Remove from heat, add butter and stir until dissolved. Add soda and salt, stirring vigorously. Pour out on a buttered slab and spread as thinly as possible. Break or cut into pieces when cool. Makes about 50 pieces.

OPAL'S BEST BUTTERSCOTCH

Try dropping from a candy funnel to get uniform melt-in-your-mouth butterscotch patties.

2½ c. sugar
½ c. light corn syrup
¾ c. water
¼ c. honey
1 c. butter
½ t. salt
½ t. rum flavoring

In a heavy saucepan, combine sugar, syrup, and water. Cover tightly and bring to a rolling boil. Remove cover, place thermometer in pan and cook without stirring to 270°. Add honey, butter, salt, and flavoring. Cook to 290°, stirring constantly. Remove from heat and pour into a 12 x 16-inch buttered jelly roll pan. Set aside to cool to a soft set. Remove to a buttered flat surface and score in 1-inch squares. When hard, break into pieces. Store airtight. Makes about 192 small pieces.

OTHER CANDY

ALMOND NOUGAT

A delicious chewy candy which can be wrapped or dipped in chocolate.

2 c. sugar
½ c. light corn syrup
½ c. water
2 T. butter
⅓ c. liquid non-dairy coffee
    cream
1 t. vanilla
1 c. blanched toasted almonds
2 T. marshmallow creme
    Confectioners' sugar
    Dipping chocolate (optional)

Combine sugar, syrup and water in heavy saucepan. Cover tightly and bring to a rolling boil. Remove lid, place thermometer in pan and cook to 270°. Remove from heat; add butter and coffee cream. Cook to 240°. Cool to about 160°; add vanilla. Beat by hand or on low speed of mixer until creamy. Add nuts and marshmallow creme. Mix together and pour into a buttered 9-inch square pan, which has been dusted with confectioners' sugar. Cover top with confectioners' sugar and let stand in cold place. Cut and wrap, dip in chocolate, or flavor and color as desired. Makes about 64 pieces.

TAFFY

Plain, old-fashioned taffy to flavor and color many ways.

2 c. sugar
2 T. cornstarch
1 c. light corn syrup
¾ c. water
1 t. salt
2 T. margarine
¼ t. any flavoring oil
    Food color as desired

In a heavy saucepan, mix together sugar and cornstarch. Stir in corn syrup, water, salt, and margarine. Place over medium heat and stir until sugar dissolves. Cover pan and bring to a boil for 2 or 3 minutes. Uncover, place thermometer in pan and cook to 266°. Remove from heat and add flavoring and food color. Stir gently, pour on a greased marble slab or a shallow greased pan to cool. When cool enough to handle, grease hands and pull until light in color and has a satiny gloss. Pull into a long rope, cut with scissors and wrap in waxed paper squares, twisting ends. Makes about 50 pieces.

MARZIPAN

- 1 c. almond paste
- 2 egg whites, unbeaten
- 3 c. confectioners' sugar
- ½ t. vanilla or rum flavoring
  Paste food color (p. 20)*

Place almond paste in a bowl and knead until soft. Add egg whites and mix well. Add confectioners' sugar one cup at a time. Continue kneading and add flavoring; marzipan should feel like heavy pie dough. Use confectioners' sugar when dusting table to prevent marzipan from sticking. Color with paste color. Mold by hand. Touch up with paste food color where necessary. Makes about 30 pieces.

Note: Use yellow color for bananas and pears, orange for carrots and pumpkins, red for strawberries and apples, and purple for plums and grapes. Make potatoes white and dust with cocoa.

MOLDED CHOCOLATE COVERED CHERRIES

Milk or semisweet chocolate coating
- 3 c. dry fondant (p. 20)*
- 2 T. liquid from cherries
- 90 small maraschino cherries

Melt sweet or semisweet chocolate flavored coating in a double boiler. Using a half-inch, good quality brush, brush molds with chocolate, checking for weak spots by holding the molds toward a light. Chill the chocolate lined molds in the freezer. While they are hardening, mix a small amount of juice from the maraschino cherries with dry fondant to form a heavy liquid. Fill the chocolate covered molds about half full of the liquid. Drop a cherry into the liquid, and seal with more melted chocolate. Make sure before you seal the molds with chocolate, there is a small rim of chocolate not covered by the liquid. Makes 90 cherries.

NO-COOK MARSHMALLOW

- ½ c. cold water
- 4 T. unflavored gelatin
- ½ c. warm water
- 2½ c. sugar
- 1½ c. invert sugar
- ¾ c. light corn syrup
- 1 t. vanilla

Soak gelatin in cold water and set aside. In a saucepan, combine warm water, sugar, and invert sugar. Heat, but do not boil. Pour into a mixing bowl and add gelatin, corn syrup, and vanilla. Whip until white and doubled in bulk. Pour into a buttered 12 x 18-inch pan and let set 24 hours before cutting. Squares may be rolled in toasted coconut, dipped in chocolate, or rolled in confectioners' sugar. Makes about 100 pieces.

Ideals also publishes a complete line of full size —8½" x 11"—collector cookbooks featuring 64 pages of over 200 recipes with beautiful color photography throughout.

Ideals cookbooks are priced at $2.95 each and can be purchased in leading book and department stores or may be ordered directly from Ideals. Enclose $2.95 per title, plus 50¢ for postage and handling to Ideals Publishing Corporation, c/o Dept. JK, 11315 Watertown Plank Rd., Milwaukee, Wisconsin 53226.

All Holidays Cookbook
American Cookbook
Barbecue Cookbook
Candy Cookbook
Christmas Cookbook
Christmas Gifts from the Kitchen
Cookie Cookbook
Country Bread Cookbook
Country Kitchen Cookbook
Family Cookbook
Farmhouse Cookbook
Festive Party Cookbook
Fish and Seafood Cookbook
From Mama's Honey Jar
From Mama's Kitchen
Gourmet Appetizer Cookbook
Gourmet on the Go
Gourmet Touch
Guide to Microwave Cooking
Have a Gourmet Christmas
Junior Chef Cookbook
Meatless Meals Cookbook
Menus from Around the World
Naturally Nutritious
Nice and Easy Desserts
Simply Delicious
Soups for All Seasons
Tempting Treasures
Whole Grain Cookbook

Additional Gifts from the Kitchen Cookbooks may be ordered at a price of $1.00 per cookbook, plus 50¢ postage and handling.

All Holidays Cookbook
Barbecue Cookbook
From Mama's Kitchen
Gourmet Touch Cookbook
Nice and Easy Desserts

Cover photograph:
Cocoa Fudge, p. 13

This is a commercial product sold in cake decorating stores.

Editorial Director, James Kuse
Managing Editor, Ralph Luedtke
Production Editor/Manager, Richard Lawson
Photographic Editor, Gerald Koser
Copy Editor, Sharon Style
Designed by, Michele Arrieh